IMAGINED HOPE

Or Chasing Shadows?

Ralph McCall

Think Deep! Series

destinée

COPYRIGHT

Imagined Hope: Or Chasing Shadows
By Ralph McCall

Published by Destinee Media, www.destineemedia.com
Written by Ralph McCall

ISBN: 978-1-938367-94-6

CONTENTS

THINK DEEP! SERIES

Imagined Hope is part of the **Think Deep! Series**, created for those who want more than surface answers.

Each book in the series explores the big questions about culture, identity, and faith—designed for a digital generation immersed in an endless array of perspectives and ever-shifting narratives.

To develop true and just discernment.

INTRODUCTION: CHASING AFTER THE WIND

"I have seen all the things that are done under the sun; all of them are meaningless, a chasing after the wind." — Ecclesiastes 1:14

You didn't start the New Age journey to be trendy. You were looking for peace. For healing. For something real.

Maybe your friends were into it. Maybe you saw something on social media, or read a book, or joined a retreat. You became curious. Then you stepped in.

You perceived what looked like beauty—the candles, the breathwork, the affirmations. You felt the resonance—the language of healing, the rituals of empowerment, the promise of awakening. And for a while, it seemed to work. You felt lighter. You felt seen.

You Imagined Hope.

But then came the ache.

Not the ache of failure, but the ache of contradiction.

You were promised a door to heaven, fulfillment, but it turned out to be a back door that led to something else instead.

You were told you were divine—but you still felt fragile.

You were told your pain was sacred—but it still hurt.

You were told you were ascending—but you still felt stuck, even trapped.

It felt like you were chasing shadows.

This book is for those who've walked the spiral. Who've done the yoga, pulled the cards, drunk the cacao, and still found themselves asking: *Is this it?*

It's not a takedown. It's a diagnosis. Not a dismissal—but a deeper invitation.

New Age spirituality is a masterclass in emotional resonance. It borrows from everywhere—Hinduism, Buddhism, psychology, mysticism, quantum physics, spirit worship, and Christianity. Then it blends them into a shimmering mosaic of self-discovery. You package what you want. But **beneath the shimmer lies a pattern: self as source, endless upgrading, and spiritual consumerism**.

You'll hear terms like **activation**, **downloads**, **ascension**, and **soul evolution**—language that promises transformation but often delivers pressure. You'll encounter ideas like **monism** ("all is one") and **pantheism** (God is everything), which sound poetic but quietly erase the personal God who speaks, loves, and rescues.

You'll see how **spiritual bypassing**—the use of rituals and "high vibes" to avoid real pain—leaves people stuck in cycles of emotional suppression. You'll notice how **aesthetic spirituality** transforms crystals, tarot, and astrology into curated content for social media, where enlightenment becomes a vibe to post, not a truth to live by.

You'll hear authentic voices. You'll see lived practices. You'll recognize the slogans. And you'll discover that the ache beneath the awakening isn't failure—it's a signal. A signal that you were made for something more than self-curated divinity.

You were made for grace.

PART I: THE PHILOSOPHICAL ACHE

Welcome to the Root Cause. You know that feeling—the low-key, persistent restlessness? That's the ache. Before you signed up for the workshops or downloaded the apps, a foundational confusion about who you are, what's real, and why pain exists was already there.

In this section, we're not talking crystals; we're talking about the **big questions** and the low-key **philosophical fault lines** that make the New Age journey so appealing. It's time to figure out what you're actually searching for when you say you want a "better vibe."

In this Part, each New Age belief is compared with an alternative, one that holds to One True Way.

CHAPTER 1: THE MIRAGE OF MEANING — WHY NEW AGE FEELS SO GOOD (AT FIRST)

The Mirage Begins

Every counterfeit begins with something true. New Age spirituality doesn't start with doctrine—it starts with relief.

You're anxious. Disconnected. Burned out. Then someone offers you something that feels sacred. Breathwork slows your pulse. Sound baths release your tears. Moon rituals give rhythm to your chaos. For a moment, you feel seen.

But beneath the beauty lies an addictive loop. You align, activate, ascend. You feel the shift. Then the ache returns. So you book another retreat. Pull another card. Drink another brew. And the cycle continues.

"I signed up for a retreat that promised everything—yoga at sunrise, a life coach session before lunch, astrology readings in the afternoon, and a sound bath at night. It felt like progress, but by the end of the week, I realized I was spinning in a never-ending loop. It became a trap."

The peace feels real, but it doesn't last. The resonance is deep, but it doesn't anchor. You're chasing meaning, but it keeps moving just out of reach.

This is the mirage. It looks like healing. It feels like awakening. But it's built on repetition, not rescue. You're not being transformed—you're being maintained.

But what if the shimmer isn't the substance?

The Allure of Immediacy

The first reason the mirage feels convincing is its immediacy. Relief comes quickly, but it doesn't endure.

A sound bath leaves you in tears, but by next week, the ache returns. A moon ritual feels like the universe is speaking directly to you, but tomorrow you need another sign. The comfort fades, and the cycle spins again. It's addictive.

You're told to "trust the universe," but the universe never speaks with a name or keeps promises you can test. Instead, you're left with subtle self-reliance: if you just align, intend, and integrate enough, you can manage your destiny.

The language of "downloads" and "soul evolution" promises upgrades but delivers pressure. You're always one vibration away from breakthrough. When inner sensation becomes the compass, truth becomes a mood. It can't correct you when you drift, and it can't hold you when you break.

C.S. Lewis once warned: *"If you look for truth, you may find comfort in the end; if you look for comfort you will not get either comfort or truth—only soft soap and wishful thinking to begin, and in the end, despair."*

Comfort without truth always fades.

Spiritual Bypassing and the High-Vibe Trap

But immediacy isn't the only hook. New Age also offers a way to avoid pain without ever facing it.

You're told to "raise your vibration," "stay positive," and "release what no longer serves you." But sometimes what you need isn't release—it's honesty.

Breathwork, cacao ceremonies, and affirmations can gratify. But when they're used to mask grief, suppress anger, or avoid trauma, they become emotional detours. You're not healing—you're bypassing.

The obsession with "high-vibe" and "low-vibe" labels creates spiritual elitism. Struggling? You're low-vibe. Glowing? You're high-vibe. It sounds empowering, but it judges not your character, but your frequency.

Christianity offers something different. It doesn't bypass pain—it meets you in it.

"Come to me, all you who are weary and burdened, and I will give you rest." — Matthew 11:28 (NIV)

The Loop of Lives — Reincarnation and Karma

Beyond bypassing, the system itself is designed to delay resolution. Karma and reincarnation stretch peace into the next life, always just out of reach.

You're told you're "clearing," "evolving," "integrating," and "paying off" unseen debts. The logic sounds just: mistakes generate karma; growth requires lifetimes; progress is incremental and earned. But karma offers fairness without forgiveness.

The scale may be balanced, but your heart is never relieved. If your current pain is payment for past-life errors, suffering becomes moral math. You are always behind, never held.

The Gospel breaks this economic model. It announces a single earthly life of real dignity, a final judgment in which justice matters, and a cross where mercy triumphs without denying truth.

"For Christ also suffered once for sins, the righteous for the unrighteous, to bring you to God." — 1 Peter 3:18 (NIV)

Karma says, "Keep paying." Grace says, "Paid in full."

The Marketplace of Meaning

And while you wait, the marketplace steps in. Coaches, healers, and retreats offer breakthrough after breakthrough—for a price.

The promise is always the same: "You're almost there." The goalposts keep moving. Identity becomes curated. Healing becomes content. Spiritual life becomes a subscription.

How much have you spent on New Age services like retreats, meditations, life coaches, divinations, energy healing, and the multitude of other practices offered? Are the enlightened experts there for your benefit, or for their own financial gain? Just asking.

Belonging depends on alignment, not love. When your vibe changes, your place does too.

Christianity answers with covenant over commerce. You don't buy access; you're adopted. You don't earn belonging; you're welcomed.

"See what great love the Father has lavished on us, that we should be called children of God! And that is what we are!" — 1 John 3:1 (NIV)

We will delve much deeper into the subject of the New Age Marketplace in a later chapter titled "Ascension Economics."

Fragments vs. Coherence

Even the ideas themselves don't hold together. What looks like a tapestry of wisdom is often a patchwork of contradictions. Technically, it's called syncretism.

"Jesus is the truth" sits beside "truth is fluid." "All paths lead" stands next to "this activation is essential." When incompatible claims merge, coherence collapses.

Human Design, Gene Keys, Enneagrams—they promise to decode your essence. At first, the categories feel profound. But the systems contradict each other, leaving you with fragments of identity rather than a coherent story.

The Gospel is not another fragment. It's a coherent story: Creator distinct from creation; humans bearing His image but not His essence; truth revealed and embodied; grace that heals and justice that stands.

"In the beginning was the Word, and the Word was with God, and the Word was God." — John 1:1 (ESV)

Fragments confuse. Coherence frees.

The Shift

You were told you're almost there. You were told you can clear it. You were told the light is within.

But what if peace doesn't arrive at the end of your effort? What if you don't need another life? What if truth isn't a vibe? It's a voice that knows your name?

The shimmer may feel real, but it cannot sustain you. The Gospel offers substance: not a cycle, but a cross. Not endless striving, but finished grace. Not a mirage, but living water.

“Whoever drinks the water I give them will never thirst. Indeed, the water I give them will become in them a spring of water welling up to eternal life.” — John 4:14 (NIV)

You’ve seen the glow of the desert heat. Now it’s time to turn toward the well.

CHAPTER 2: TRUTH WARS — RELATIVISM VS. REVELATION

Introduction: The Quicksand of "Your Truth"

You've heard it everywhere: "Live your truth." "What's true for you might not be true for me." "There's no one right way."

It sounds compassionate. Inclusive. Empowering.

But it's also the philosophical equivalent of quicksand. Relativism feels freeing—until you need something solid to stand on.

"I once sat in a 'truth circle' where everyone shared their perspective. One person said the universe is impersonal energy. Another said it's a loving mother. Another said Jesus is just one of many guides. Ultimately, the facilitator smiled and said, "All of these are true." For a moment, it felt inclusive. But later I realized—if everything is true, then nothing can be trusted."

What happens when every truth cancels the others out?

The Collapse of Meaning

Relativism promises liberation, but it quietly erodes the very idea of truth. It replaces reality with preference. It swaps coherence for comfort.

Philosopher Allan Bloom warned: *"The danger... is not error but indifference to truth."*

In a relativistic world, truth becomes a mirror—not a compass. You see yourself, but you can't orient yourself.

This is why so many feel spiritually exhausted. We crave authenticity, but we've been taught that nothing is objectively real. We want to "find ourselves," but we've been told there's no fixed self to find.

Truth becomes a mirror, not a compass. But a compass is what we need.

Human Design and the Mirror Effect

Human Design coaching works similarly. You're given a chart that claims to reveal your essence—your type, your strategy, your inner authority. At first, it feels profound. You finally have a map.

But the map often reflects what you already believe. And if it doesn't, you're told to "take what resonates and leave the rest." The system becomes a mirror, not a compass.

"I loved my Human Design reading. It felt like someone finally understood me. But when I got a second reading from a different coach, it contradicted the first. I realized I was just picking the version that made me feel good."

Truth becomes a vibe. A preference. A curated identity.

But when life falls apart, vibes don't hold you. Preferences don't rescue you.

"Your word is a lamp to my feet and a light to my path." — Psalm 119:105 (ESV)

The Return of Gnosticism

This isn't new. The early church faced a similar challenge in the form of Gnosticism—a movement that claimed salvation came through hidden knowledge (gnosis) available only to the enlightened.

Today's "downloads," "activations," and "hidden teachings" echo the same pattern. One person's "download" may contradict another's, yet both are affirmed as equally valid.

The allure of secret knowledge flatters the ego: you're special, you're chosen, you've unlocked what others can't see. But it also isolates, fragments, and deceives.

Philip J. Lee observed: *"The hunger for hidden wisdom is as old as humanity, but it always divides rather than unites."*

The Gospel is the opposite of Gnosticism. It's not hidden—it's revealed. Not secret—but public. Not abstract—but incarnate.

Revelation vs. Spiritual Pluralism

Many New Age seekers try to harmonize relativism with revelation. They treat Jesus as one enlightened master among many. His claims get reduced to metaphor or mysticism. But this creates cognitive dissonance.

If Jesus is who He says He is—the incarnate Logos, the exclusive way to God—then He cannot be one truth among many. He must be either the Truth or a lie.

Francis Schaeffer put it plainly: *"Christianity is not just religious truth. It is total truth—truth about the whole of reality."*

If Jesus is who He says He is, can He really be just one option among many?

Digital Spirituality and the Aesthetic Trap

On social media, truth is often replaced by aesthetic spirituality—crystals, tarot spreads, moon rituals, and affirmations curated for visual impact. It's not just about belief—it's about branding. Enlightenment becomes a vibe to post.

Spiritual influencers—coaches, gurus, and healers—gain followers by blending traditions, speaking in poetic generalities, and offering emotional resonance. But their authority is built on personal experience, not transcendent truth. Their teachings shift with trends, and their wisdom often contradicts itself.

"I followed a spiritual coach who quoted Jesus, Buddha, and quantum physics in the same breath. It felt deep, but eventually I realized—it was just nice words. No coherence. No anchor."

"Jesus Christ is the same yesterday and today and forever." — Hebrews 13:8 (NIV)

The Shift

You don't need hidden codes. You don't need secret downloads. You don't need "your truth."

What if truth isn't a feeling, but a voice? What if it isn't hidden, but revealed? What if it isn't fragile, but unchanging?

You need the Truth. Not concealed. Revealed. Not abstract. Incarnate. Not a mood. A Person.

"Then you will know the truth, and the truth will set you free." — John 8:32 (NIV)

CHAPTER 3: THE GOD WITHIN — WHY YOU'RE NOT DIVINE (AND THAT'S GOOD NEWS)

The Rise of Sacred Narcissism

You've probably heard it: "I am God." "The divine is within me." "We are all expressions of Source."

It sounds empowering. It feels sacred. It even borrows Christian language—"made in God's image"—but flips the meaning.

Instead of being created by God, you become God. Instead of worship, you self-actualize. Instead of surrender, you ascend.

At first, this message feels healing. If you've been shamed, ignored, or abused, being told you are divine feels like restoration. You're not broken—you're powerful. You're not small—you're sacred.

But over time, the message shifts. You're not just valuable—you're ultimate. You're not just loved—you're the source of love. You're not just created—you're the Creator.

"I used to say 'I am divine' every morning in the mirror. It helped me feel strong. But eventually, I started to feel pressure. If I'm divine, why do I still feel so weak? Why doesn't the universe obey my commands?"

This is sacred narcissism: self-worship dressed in spiritual language.

What happens when the god you're told to worship is yourself—and you can't carry the weight?

Pantheism, Monism, and the Collapse of Distinction

Philosophically, this idea comes from **pantheism** (the belief that God is everything) and **monism** (the belief that all is one). These frameworks dissolve the boundary between Creator and creation. They spiritualize the self, sacralize nature, and flatten transcendence into immanence.

But in doing so, they erase the very distinction that makes worship possible.

If everything is divine, then nothing is. If you are God, then there is no one higher to guide, correct, or redeem you.

Theologian Peter Jones warns that this collapse of categories is not liberation but confusion: *"When all distinctions are erased, truth and falsehood, good and evil, God and creation all blur into one. And when everything is sacred, nothing is."*

Christ Consciousness and the Redefinition of Jesus

This is where the popular teaching of "Christ Consciousness" comes in. In meditation groups, Reiki circles, or channeling sessions, Jesus is often redefined—not as the incarnate Son of God who entered history, but as a universal energy or state of awareness that anyone can "activate."

The message is: "You don't need a Savior—you just need to awaken to your inner Christ."

At first, it sounds inclusive and spiritual. It even borrows Christian language, which makes it feel safe. But look closer: it collapses the distinction between Creator and creation. Instead of Christ being unique, He becomes a metaphor for what you already are. Instead of grace, you just "level up."

If Jesus is only a symbol of what you already are, then who rescues you when you break?

Kundalini and the Theology of Awakening

Kundalini yoga offers another vivid example. Practitioners are told that a coiled divine energy lies dormant at the base of the spine, waiting to be awakened. As it rises through the chakras, you are said to realize your true nature as God.

The sensations can feel electric—tingling, euphoric, transcendent. But beneath the experience is a theology of self-divinization: salvation is not something you receive, but something you awaken within yourself.

This is the language of activation and downloads—terms that promise spiritual upgrades and inner divinity. You're not being rescued—you're being revealed.

But what if the self you reveal is still fragile, still anxious, still limited?

Monism: The Collapse of Everything

Beneath pantheism lies monism—the belief that all distinctions are illusions. Good and evil, truth and error, Creator and creation—all are ultimately "one."

This sounds profound, but it erases moral clarity. If all is one, then evil is just misalignment. Sin is just ignorance. Darkness is just another shade of light.

But Scripture insists otherwise:

"Woe to those who call evil good and good evil." — Isaiah 5:20 (NIV)

Monism collapses categories; Christianity clarifies them. God is distinct from creation. Good is distinct from evil. Truth is different from lies.

And that distinction is not oppressive—it's liberating. Because it means evil can be named, confronted, and overcome. It means justice is real, and mercy is meaningful.

The Danger of Self-Deification

When you believe you are divine, suffering becomes a threat to your identity. Weakness feels like failure. Dependence feels like regression. You begin to chase perfection, not peace.

This is why so many New Age practices lean on mirror affirmations. You're told to stand in front of your reflection and repeat: "I am divine. I am unlimited. I am Source."

At first, it feels empowering—especially if you've battled shame or insecurity. But over time, it creates pressure.

The very words meant to free you can become chains.

The Collapse of Worship

Believing "I am God" doesn't just distort theology—it dismantles worship in practice.

- **From worship to branding**: When Jesus is redefined from Savior to symbol—"Christ Consciousness" as awareness rather than a Person—you don't need grace. You just need awakening. Jesus becomes a mirror for your own potential rather than a Master who calls you to follow.
- **The weight of divinity**: If you are God, weakness equals failure, dependence equals regression, and suffering equals contradiction. You begin performing divinity—activating, aligning, ascending—because rest looks like defeat. The result isn't freedom; it's pressure.

- **When life breaks you**: This theology breaks too. The self you enthroned cannot carry you. The god you tried to be cannot save you.

The Shift

You were told you are divine. You were told you are unlimited. You were told you are Source. By the way, wasn't that belief the first sin in the Garden of Eden?

But what if you don't need to be God—you need to be loved by Him? What if you don't need to ascend—you need Someone who descends? What if you don't need to awaken to your own light—you need the Light of the world to call your name?

You are not divine. You are designed. You are not the source. You are the image. You are not everything. You are loved by the One who is.

"Come to me, all you who are weary and burdened, and I will give you rest." — Matthew 11:28 (NIV)

CHAPTER 4: SACRED PAIN? — WHY SUFFERING ISN'T YOUR TEACHER

Introduction: When Pain Gets Spiritualized

You've probably heard it: "Your wounds are your wisdom." "Pain is your portal." "Your trauma is your teacher."

It sounds noble. It feels profound. It gives meaning to your suffering.

But it also distorts reality. You're not just hurting—you're spiritualizing your hurt. You're not just processing—you're glorifying pain. And that changes everything.

The Glorification of Brokenness

In many New Age circles, suffering is reframed as sacred initiation. The darker the night, the deeper the wisdom. The heavier the trauma, the higher the potential for awakening.

This is why plant medicine ceremonies—like ayahuasca or San Pedro—are often described as "teachers." Participants are told their trauma will reveal hidden wisdom through visions. The vomiting, the terror, the disorientation—all are interpreted as sacred lessons. Pain itself becomes the curriculum.

"I drank the brew and was told the visions would show me my wounds as portals. But when the ceremony ended, the ache was still there—only now it was spiritualized. And I felt exhausted."

The logic is seductive: if your suffering is sacred, then you don't have to face its rawness—you can reframe it as progress. But the wound remains.

What if pain isn't a portal, but a signal that you need healing?

The Dark Night After the Glow

This is the setup for what many former New Age seekers call **the *dark night of the soul*—the emotional crash that follows the glow.** After the rituals fade and the resonance wears off, you're left with the same ache, only now it's dressed in spiritual language.

You feel disoriented, hollow, and confused. You wonder if you've been chasing healing or just bypassing it.

Rituals of Bypassing

Spiritual bypassing shows up in rituals that promise heart-opening but avoid heart-healing.

- **Cacao ceremonies**: Participants drink the bitter brew, sit in a circle, and are told that the tears, the heaviness, the discomfort are signs of "heart-opening." The pain is interpreted as proof of depth.
- **Sweat lodges**: The heat, the suffocation, the struggle to endure are framed as spiritual purification. The more you suffer, the more you are told you are being cleansed.

But this is not redemption—it's ritualized masochism. Pain is endlessly reinterpreted, never truly healed.

As psychologist Ronald Siegel notes, *"The pursuit of peak experiences can become addictive. When the high fades, people often feel more lost than before."*

The Cross vs. the Circle

The difference is not whether suffering matters, but what suffering means.

In the New Age, pain is a circle—you go inward, reinterpret, endure. In Christianity, pain is a cross—you bring it to Jesus, who bore it for you.

The apostle Paul doesn't say, "Your trauma will save you." He says:

"Christ Jesus came into the world to save sinners." — 1 Timothy 1:15 (NIV)

The cross doesn't romanticize pain. It redeems it. It doesn't turn wounds into wisdom. It turns wounds into scars—healed, but still visible, testifying to grace.

The Shift

You don't need to glorify your pain. You don't need to drink it, sweat it, or spiritualize it. You need to bring it to the One who already carried it.

What if your wounds aren't teachers, but burdens you were never meant to carry alone? What if your scars don't define you, but point to a deeper healing? What if suffering isn't sacred, but redeemable?

The shimmer of sacred pain fades. The cross endures.

"He heals the brokenhearted and binds up their wounds." — Psalm 147:3 (NIV)

CHAPTER 5: ASCENSION ECONOMICS — WHY SPIRITUAL GROWTH ISN'T A SUBSCRIPTION

Introduction: The Price of Progress

You've probably heard it: "Invest in your healing." "Upgrade your frequency." "Your next breakthrough is just one activation away."

It sounds empowering. It feels intentional. It borrows the language of growth and stewardship. But underneath the affirmations lies a system—one that looks less like transformation and more like a marketplace.

The Cost of Enlightenment

New Age spirituality often presents itself as a path of freedom. But for many, it becomes a cycle of spending. Retreats, workshops, energy healings, life coaches, moon ceremonies, and sacred sexuality intensives—each one promises the next level. Each one comes with a price tag.

"I spent thousands on spiritual coaching, tantra sessions, and energy work. I kept thinking, 'This next one will unlock everything.' But I just felt more anxious—and more broke."

The logic is subtle: if you're not healed, you haven't invested enough. If you're still stuck, you need a higher-tier experience. Spiritual growth becomes a subscription—renewed monthly, upgraded annually, never complete.

What if the real cost isn't financial, but emotional exhaustion?

The Pressure to Perform

In this system, your spiritual worth is tied to your progress. You're told to "do the work," "clear your blocks," and "align with abundance." But the work never ends. The blocks keep multiplying. And abundance always seems just out of reach.

You're not resting—you're managing. You're not being loved—you're being optimized. You're not being transformed—you're being maintained.

And when the glow fades, you're told it's your fault. Your vibration dropped. Your aura's blocked. Your karma isn't cleared. So you book another session. Buy another crystal. Sign up for another course.

The cycle continues. The cost increases. The peace never lasts.

Tim Keller once observed: *"If you center your life on yourself, your own comfort and happiness, you will never find satisfaction or significance."*

Spiritual Consumerism and the Illusion of Progress

New Age spirituality often blends healing with branding. Coaches and influencers curate their offerings with poetic language and aesthetic visuals. You're not just buying a service—you're buying a story. A lifestyle. A vibe.

But behind the curated content is a business model. The promise is always the same: "You're almost there." The goalposts keep moving. Identity becomes curated. Healing becomes content.

"I followed a spiritual influencer who offered 'divine embodiment coaching.' Her posts were beautiful. Her words were powerful. But after three sessions, I realized—I wasn't being healed. I was being sold a feeling."

Consumer spirituality doesn't transform you—it markets to you.

Karma and the Economics of Delay

Many New Age systems are built on karmic logic. You're told that pain is payment for past-life mistakes. That growth takes lifetimes. That breakthrough must be earned.

At first, this sounds fair. But over time, it becomes exhausting.

You're always behind. You're always clearing. You're always waiting.

Karma offers fairness without forgiveness. You can improve your standing, but you can't be absolved. Justice stays abstract. Shame lingers underground. And if peace is always "next life," then hope is always postponed.

The prophet Jeremiah described this futility long ago:

"My people have committed two evils: they have forsaken me, the fountain of living waters, and hewed out cisterns for themselves, broken cisterns that can hold no water." — Jeremiah 2:13 (ESV)

The Gospel and the Gift of Grace

Christianity offers something different. It doesn't sell healing—it gives it. It doesn't charge for access—it adopts you. It doesn't ask you to ascend—it descends.

Jesus doesn't say, "You're almost there." He says:

"It is finished." — John 19:30 (NIV)

The Gospel breaks the economic model. Instead of lifetimes of clearing, you're given a clean slate. Instead of spiritual subscriptions, you're given a Savior. Instead of karma, you're given grace.

And grace doesn't run out.

The Shift

You don't need another upgrade. You don't need another activation. You don't need another payment plan for peace.

What if the breakthrough you're chasing isn't something you buy, but something you receive? What if the freedom you long for isn't a subscription, but a gift?

You don't need ascension economics. You need grace.

PART II: THE CYCLE OF SHADOWS

You bought the ticket and took the ride. Now what? This section is the deep dive into the **actual practices**—from manifestation and energy healing to astrology, psychedelics, and past-life regressions.

We're unpacking the tools you use to pursue that "expected freedom." We'll show you exactly why these methods create an **endless, exhausting cycle** where you're always one affirmation, one retreat, or one "download" away from the finish line. Spoiler: The shimmer is high-key unsustainable.

Each practice is contrasted with a different lifestyle, a belief in One True God.

Perhaps you have had enough of the "actual practices" and no longer want to think about them. Now you wish to learn more about the Christian alternative. If that's the case, jump forward to Part III.

CHAPTER 6: "IT'S MY TRUTH" — WHY SUBJECTIVE SPIRITUALITY CAN'T SAVE YOU

Introduction: The Age of "My Truth"

You've heard it everywhere: "Speak your truth." "Honor your truth." "Live your truth."

It sounds empowering. It feels authentic. It gives you permission to be yourself.

But it also creates confusion. If everyone has their own truth, then truth becomes a mood. A vibe. A personal brand. And when truth is personalized, it loses its power to challenge, correct, or rescue.

What happens when your truth collides with someone else's?

The Rise of Expressive Individualism

The phrase "my truth" comes from **expressive individualism**—the belief that identity is discovered by looking inward and expressing outward. Philosopher Charles Taylor calls this "the culture of authenticity," where meaning is self-generated and morality is self-defined.

In this framework, truth is no longer something external to be discovered—it's something internal to be curated. But this creates a paradox:

- If truth is whatever you feel, it can't guide you when your feelings change.
- If truth is whatever you want, it can't confront you when you're wrong.

Truth becomes fragile, shifting with your mood. And when life breaks you, "my truth" breaks with it.

Os Guinness warns: *"Far from being a naïve and reactionary notion, truth is one of the simplest, most precious gifts without which we would not be able to handle reality or negotiate life."*

Vibe Morality and the High-Frequency Trap

On social media, truth is often filtered through aura culture—a world where people and experiences are labeled as "high-vibe" or "low-vibe."

If someone's energy feels good, they're elevated. If they're struggling, they're dismissed.

This sounds empowering, but it creates spiritual elitism. You're judged not by your character, but by your frequency. And if your vibe drops, your worth feels like it drops too.

This is especially damaging for those dealing with anxiety, grief, or trauma. Instead of being supported, they're told to "raise their vibration." Instead of being comforted, they're told they're "low-vibe." Pain becomes a performance issue.

What if truth isn't about frequency at all, but about faithfulness?

The Return of Gnosticism

This obsession with "hidden truths" isn't new. The early church faced the same challenge in **Gnosticism**—a movement that claimed salvation came through secret knowledge available only to the enlightened.

Today's "downloads," "activations," and "hidden teachings" echo the same pattern. They flatter the ego: you're special, you're chosen, you've unlocked what others can't see. But they also isolate, fragment, and deceive.

Philip J. Lee observed: *"The hunger for hidden wisdom is as old as humanity, but it always divides rather than unites."*

The Gospel and Objective Truth

Christianity doesn't offer "your truth." It offers **the truth**.

Not a mood. Not a mirror. Not a brand.

Truth that can correct you when you drift. Truth that can hold you when you break. Truth that doesn't change when your feelings do.

Jesus doesn't say, "Find your truth." He says:

"Then you will know the truth, and the truth will set you free." — John 8:32 (NIV)

That's not arrogance. It's clarity. It's not exclusion. It's invitation. Because when truth is a Person, it's not just a concept to debate—it's a voice that knows your name.

The Shift

You don't need a mirror. You need a compass. You don't need a vibe. You need a voice. You don't need "your truth." You need the Truth.

And the Truth isn't fragile. He isn't shifting. He isn't hidden. He is steady. He is revealed. He is here.

CHAPTER 7: MANIFESTATION AND THE LAW OF ATTRACTION — WHY YOU CAN'T SPEAK THE UNIVERSE INTO SERVING YOU

Introduction: The Promise of Control

You've seen it everywhere: "Manifest it." "Speak it." "Call it in."

The promise is seductively simple—align your thoughts and emotions, and the universe will deliver your desires. It looks like hope but often functions like control. When life feels chaotic, manifestation offers a lever. Pull it right, and reality will obey.

But what happens when the lever breaks?

The Emotional Appeal and Hidden Pressure

Manifestation feels empowering because it gives you a sense of agency.

- **Relief**: In a world of uncertainty, manifestation feels like control.
- **Ritual**: Vision boards, affirmations, scripting—they give shape to your longing.
- **Loop**: But when results don't come, the blame turns inward. "I didn't visualize enough." "My vibration slipped." Hope becomes performance, and desire becomes anxiety.

"I paid for a manifestation masterclass that promised a 'money breakthrough.' I journaled, declared, and visualized. The only thing that really increased was my stress—and my credit card balance."

C.S. Lewis once noted the crucial difference between prayer and magic: *"For magic and applied science alike the goal is power over nature."* Prayer submits; magic controls.

Why It Collapses: Control That Can't Carry You

Manifestation often collapses under its own weight.

- **Selective memory**: Wins get spiritualized; losses get rationalized. We notice "hits," forget "misses," and call it proof.
- **Ethical fog**: If reality is malleable to desire, what happens when your desire harms others? Without a moral anchor, power outruns wisdom.
- **Spiritual bypass**: Declaring abundance can mute lament. Naming it "alignment" can hide avoidance. Pain needs presence, not positivity.

"When my mom got sick, I tried to manifest her healing. I visualized, declared, and raised my vibration. But when she didn't get better, I felt crushing guilt. People told me I must not have believed enough. Instead of comfort, manifestation left me with shame."

What kind of hope leaves you feeling guilty for grieving?

The Biblical Contrast: Providence, Prayer, and Peace

The Bible offers a different vision of reality—one rooted not in projection, but in providence.

- **Providence over projection**:
- **Prayer over scripting**:
- **Trust over control**:

Manifestation says reality answers to your voice. The Gospel says your voice is heard by a Father.

The Shift

You don't need to declare outcomes. You don't need to manage vibrations. You don't need to bend the universe to your will.

What if peace comes not from control, but from trust? What if freedom comes not from scripting reality, but from surrendering to the One who holds it?

From "make it happen" to "Your kingdom come." From vibration management to honest lament and steady prayer. From chasing control to receiving care.

CHAPTER 8: WRITTEN IN THE STARS — WHY ASTROLOGY CAN'T DEFINE YOU

Introduction: The Pull of the Zodiac

You've seen it everywhere: "What's your sign?" "Mercury's in retrograde." "Your chart explains everything."

Astrology promises clarity. It gives you categories, language, and a sense of belonging. It feels ancient, mystical, and personal.

But beneath the poetry lies a problem: the stars may inspire wonder, but they cannot define your worth.

The Comfort of Categories

Astrology appeals because it offers identity. Instead of drifting, you're anchored in a sign. Instead of randomness, you're given a pattern.

"I used to check my horoscope every morning. It gave me a sense of control—like the universe was whispering guidance just for me. But when the predictions didn't match reality, I felt more confused than before."

The categories comfort, but they also confine. You're told who you are before you've even lived it.

What happens when your chart feels like a cage instead of a compass?

The Problem of Contradictions

Astrology thrives on generalities. Horoscopes are written to resonate with almost anyone.

- "You're independent but crave connection."
- "You're creative but need structure."
- "You're sensitive but strong."

These statements feel true because they're broad enough to fit most people. Psychologists call this the **Barnum effect**—the tendency to accept vague, flattering statements as uniquely personal.

The result? You feel seen, but not really known.

The Weight of Determinism

Astrology also carries a hidden burden: determinism. If your chart dictates your personality, your struggles, and your future, then freedom shrinks.

- Struggling in relationships? Blame your Venus placement.
- Feeling anxious? Blame your moon sign.
- Career stalled? Mercury retrograde.

At first, this relieves responsibility. But over time, it steals agency. You're not free—you're fated.

Philosopher Peter Kreeft once said: *"If you are merely a product of the stars, then you are less than human. But if you are made in the image of God, you are more than the stars."*

The Ancient Warning

Astrology isn't new. Ancient Israel wrestled with it too. The prophet Isaiah warned:

"Let now the astrologers, the stargazers, the monthly prognosticators, stand up and save you from what shall come upon you. Behold, they shall be as stubble; the fire shall burn them." — Isaiah 47:13–14 (KJV)

The point isn't to mock the stars—it's to remind us they are created things, not creators. They declare glory, but they don't dictate destiny.

The Gospel and True Identity

Christianity doesn't erase the wonder of the stars—it reframes it. The heavens declare God's glory, but they don't define your story.

Your worth isn't written in constellations. It's written in covenant. Your identity isn't determined by planetary alignments. It's secured by a Person.

"He determines the number of the stars and calls them each by name. Great is our Lord and mighty in power; his understanding has no limit." — Psalm 147:4–5 (NIV)

The same God who names the stars also names you.

The Shift

You don't need Mercury to guide you. You don't need your chart to define you. You don't need the stars to tell you who you are.

What if the One who made the stars also made you? What if your worth isn't written in the sky, but spoken by a voice that knows your name?

The stars inspire wonder. But they cannot save.

CHAPTER 9: ENERGY HEALING AND THE ILLUSION OF POWER — WHY VIBRATIONS CAN'T SAVE YOU

Introduction: The Promise of Invisible Power

"Your aura is blocked." "Your chakras need balancing." "Your energy field is out of alignment."

Energy healing promises what medicine can't: invisible solutions to invisible problems. It offers language for the aches you can't explain and rituals for the wounds you can't name. It feels mystical, holistic, and hopeful.

But beneath the glow lies a question: if energy is the cure, why does the ache always return?

The Appeal of Energy Healing

Energy healing resonates because it validates your experience. You feel something is wrong, but doctors can't explain it. Energy language gives you categories: blocked chakras, stagnant qi, misaligned vibrations.

"I went to a Reiki session after months of anxiety. The practitioner waved her hands over me, and I felt tingling and warmth. For a moment, I thought I was healed. But by the next week, the anxiety was back."

The sensations are real. The relief is real. But the healing is often temporary.

What if the experience is soothing, but not saving?

The Marketplace of Vibrations

Energy healing has become an industry. Reiki, crystal therapy, sound baths, aura cleanses—each one promises balance, each one comes with a price.

The logic is subtle: if you're still struggling, you need another session. If the ache returns, your energy must still be blocked. Healing becomes a subscription, not a solution.

Sociologist Paul Heelas notes: *"The New Age is less about truth and more about techniques—rituals that promise transformation but often deliver repetition."*

The Problem of Subjectivity

Energy healing relies on subjective sensations—warmth, tingling, lightness. But these experiences can be explained by psychology as much as spirituality. Placebo effects, suggestion, and expectation all play a role.

This doesn't mean the experiences are fake. It means they're fragile. Relief that depends on sensation fades when the sensation does.

If your healing depends on a feeling, what happens when the feeling disappears?

The Biblical Contrast: Power with a Name

The Bible doesn't deny invisible realities. It speaks of spirit, soul, and unseen powers. But it grounds them in a Person, not a vibration.

- **Healing with authority**:

- **Power with a name**:

Energy healing offers power without a person. Christianity offers power with a name.

The Shift

You don't need another aura cleanse. You don't need another chakra alignment. You don't need another vibration upgrade.

What if healing isn't about energy, but about encounter? What if power isn't impersonal, but personal? What if the One who spoke the universe into being can also speak peace into you?

The shimmer of vibrations fades. The Word endures.

CHAPTER 10: CHANNELING AND SPIRIT GUIDES — WHY VOICES WITHOUT ANCHORS CAN'T LEAD YOU HOME

Introduction: The Seduction of Voices

"Your guide is speaking." "The spirits have a message for you." "Channel this energy—it will show you the way."

Channeling promises intimacy with the unseen. It offers wisdom beyond yourself, direction when you feel lost, and comfort when you feel alone. It feels mystical, personal, and empowering.

But the question lingers: **what world are we stepping into?**

New Age practices don't open a neutral realm of harmless energy. They open a dark spiritual world that entraps, deceives, and torments. What begins as curiosity often ends in bondage.

The Allure of Spirit Guides

For many, spirit guides feel like companions. They promise protection, insight, and affirmation. In a world of loneliness, the idea that unseen beings are watching over you is deeply comforting.

"I went to a medium who told me my grandmother was speaking through her. She said things that felt personal, even healing. But later, I realized much of it was vague enough to apply to anyone. And then the visions and dreams that followed were terrifying."

The appeal is real. But so is the risk.

The Problem of Contradiction

Channeling sessions often produce conflicting messages. One guide says you're destined for wealth. Another warns of struggle. One says your soulmate is near. Another says you must wait lifetimes.

If all voices are valid, then none can be trusted.

Sociologist Christopher Partridge notes: *"The New Age is marked by a democratization of the spirit world—every voice is valid, every revelation is affirmed. But this inclusivity often collapses into incoherence."*

What happens when the voices you trust start to disagree?

The Dark Reality: Entrapment and Torment

Many who enter this world discover it is not filled with light, but with shadows. Reiki, for example, is often marketed as "energy healing." But countless testimonies reveal that instead of peace, people leave with nightmares, oppression, and fear. What was supposed to heal them instead opened the door to torment.

This is not surprising. The Bible teaches that evil spirits are real. They masquerade as helpers, but their goal is to enslave. What begins as curiosity can become a chain.

A Pagan Worldview of Fear

Channeling and related practices flow from a pagan worldview—one that sees nature and the unseen as forces to be appeased, energies to be balanced, and spirits to be managed. Instead of freedom, it produces fear: fear of karma, fear of curses, fear of unseen powers.

But the Bible reveals a different story: creation is not a trap to escape, but a gift to steward. Nature is not a force to fear, but a theater of God's glory. Life is not a cycle of dread, but a story with meaning.

The Biblical Warning Against Divination

The Bible doesn't treat divination as harmless curiosity. It consistently condemns it as a counterfeit source of guidance.

- **Prohibition and Condemnation**
  - *"Let no one be found among you… who practices divination or sorcery, interprets omens, engages in witchcraft, or casts spells, or who is a medium or spiritist or who consults the dead. Anyone who does these things is detestable to the Lord."* — Deuteronomy 18:10–12 (NIV)
  - *"Do not practice divination or seek omens."* — Leviticus 19:26 (NIV)
  - *"Rebellion is like the sin of divination."* — 1 Samuel 15:23 (NIV)

These passages show that divination is not just a bad habit—it is spiritual disloyalty. To seek guidance from spirits, omens, or cards is to turn away from the living God.

- **Source of Guidance** Divination is condemned because it replaces God's voice with another. Instead of prayer, it turns to omens. Instead of Scripture, it turns to symbols. Instead of the Spirit, it opens the door to spirits.
- **Spiritual Source** The Bible also reveals that some forms of divination are not just empty rituals—they are energized by dark powers. In Acts 16:16–18, a slave girl had a "spirit of

divination" that enabled her to tell fortunes. Paul cast it out, showing that the source was not neutral but demonic.

God's Seriousness: Why So Severe?

In Israel's law, divination and spiritism were not just discouraged—they carried the death penalty (Leviticus 20:6, 27).

Why so severe? Because these practices are not games. They open the door to deception, idolatry, and demonic influence. They enslave people God loves. They lead entire communities into fear and darkness.

What God calls "detestable" is not a curiosity to play with. It is a danger to flee from.

Modern Expressions of Ancient Practices

The Bible doesn't name tarot cards, oracle decks, or Human Design charts, but they fall under the same category: tools of divination.

- **Tarot and Oracle Cards**: Used to interpret symbols and predict outcomes, they function as modern omens.
- **Human Design**: Though wrapped in the language of personality and energy, it seeks to map destiny apart from God's Word.
- **Reiki and Energy Healing**: Promoted as harmless therapy, but often functioning as a channel for spiritual forces that are not from God.

From a biblical perspective, these are not harmless self-help tools. They are doorways—channels that open people to spiritual influences that are not from God.

The Danger of Disguise

Not all voices are benign. Some flatter, some deceive, some manipulate. The Bible warns that even dark powers can masquerade as light:

"Satan himself masquerades as an angel of light." — 2 Corinthians 11:14 (NIV)

This doesn't mean every spiritual experience is demonic. But it does mean discernment matters. Not every voice deserves your trust.

The Weight of Dependence

Channeling also creates dependence. Instead of learning to discern, you outsource your decisions to unseen voices. Instead of growing in wisdom, you wait for downloads. Instead of building resilience, you seek reassurance.

"I used to ask my guides about everything—relationships, jobs, even what to eat. At first it felt freeing, and even exciting to get revelations from another dimension. But eventually, I realized I couldn't make a decision without them. I wasn't empowered—I was enslaved. And the visions and nightmares were horrid."

What kind of freedom leaves you unable to choose without permission?

The Biblical Contrast: A Voice That Anchors

The Bible doesn't deny the unseen realm. It acknowledges spirits, angels, and powers. But it anchors discernment in a single voice—the voice of the Shepherd.

"My sheep listen to my voice; I know them, and they follow me."
— John 10:27 (NIV)

Unlike the shifting voices of channeling, this voice is steady. Unlike the contradictions of guides, this voice is coherent. Unlike the dependence of downloads, this voice leads to freedom.

The Shift

You don't need omens. You don't need cards. You don't need Reiki, downloads, or voices that flatter but cannot anchor.

What if the guidance you long for isn't hidden in symbols, but revealed in Scripture? What if the wisdom you seek isn't in spirits, but in the Spirit? What if the voice you need isn't counterfeit, but true?

The shimmer of divination leads to destruction. The voice of the Shepherd endures.

CHAPTER 11: PAST LIVES AND REINCARNATION — WHY ONE LIFE IS ENOUGH

Introduction: The Lure of Another Chance

“You’ve been here before.” “This explains your karma.” “Your soul is evolving through lifetimes.”

Reincarnation promises fairness. It explains suffering as payment, injustice as balance, and longing as unfinished business. It feels ancient, just, and hopeful.

But beneath the poetry lies a burden: if life is endless cycles, peace is always postponed.

The Comfort of Continuity

Reincarnation appeals because it softens the sting of death. Instead of finality, you’re given continuity. Instead of judgment, you’re given another chance.

“I was told my fear of water came from drowning in a past life. At first, it gave me comfort—like there was an explanation. But it didn’t actually help me swim. The fear remained.”

The story soothes, but it doesn’t solve.

What if the ache you feel isn’t from a past life, but from this one?

Karma: Fairness Without Forgiveness

At the heart of reincarnation is karma—the belief that every action generates consequences that ripple across lifetimes.

On the surface, it feels just. But in practice, it becomes crushing. If your suffering is punishment for past mistakes, then every hardship is your fault. Every illness, every loss, every failure becomes moral math.

Theologian Ravi Zacharias once observed: *"Karma offers no forgiveness, only consequences. Grace offers forgiveness, and with it, hope."*

The Weight of Endless Cycles

Reincarnation promises progress, but it also delays resolution. If enlightenment takes lifetimes, peace is always deferred. You're always behind, always clearing, always waiting.

Instead of freedom, you're given an endless treadmill. Instead of closure, you're given delay.

What kind of hope never arrives?

The Biblical Contrast: One Life, One Hope

The Bible offers a different vision: one life of dignity, one death of finality, one judgment of justice, and one cross of mercy.

"Just as people are destined to die once, and after that to face judgment, so Christ was sacrificed once to take away the sins of many." — Hebrews 9:27–28 (NIV)

Instead of lifetimes of clearing, you're given a clean slate. Instead of karma, you're given grace. Instead of endless cycles, you're given a decisive rescue.

The Shift

You don’t need another lifetime. You don’t need to pay off invisible debts. You don’t need to wait for peace in the next round.

What if this life is enough? What if justice and mercy meet not in cycles, but in a cross? What if hope isn’t postponed, but present?

You don’t need endless lives. You need eternal life.

CHAPTER 12: CRYSTALS AND SACRED OBJECTS — WHY POWER ISN'T IN THE STONES

Introduction: The Glow of the Stones

Rose quartz for love. Amethyst for peace. Citrine for abundance.

Crystals promise what we long for—healing, clarity, protection. They shimmer with beauty, carry ancient symbolism, and feel charged with mystery. Holding one in your hand can feel like holding hope itself.

But the question remains: if the power is in the stone, why does the ache return when you put it down?

The Comfort of Tangibility

Crystals appeal because they're tangible. Unlike abstract affirmations, they can be touched, carried, and displayed. They give form to longing.

"I wore a rose quartz necklace for months, believing it would heal my heart. At first, it gave me comfort—like I was carrying love with me. But when the relationship ended, the stone couldn't hold me. It was just a necklace."

The comfort was real, but the healing wasn't.

The Marketplace of Meaning

Crystals have become a booming industry. Shops sell them with poetic descriptions: "charged with lunar energy," "aligned with your aura," "infused with intention." Each stone is marketed as a key to unlock your destiny.

But behind the mystique is commerce. The same stone that promises transcendence is mass-mined, mass-marketed, and mass-sold.

Sociologist Paul Heelas notes: *"The New Age is less about truth and more about techniques—rituals that promise transformation but often deliver repetition."*

When healing is sold by the ounce, is it still healing—or just branding?

The Problem of Projection

Much of crystal power comes from projection. You assign meaning to the stone, and the stone reflects it back. Psychologists refer to this as the placebo effect—belief itself can produce the sensation of change.

This doesn't mean the experience is fake. It means the power isn't in the stone—it's in the story you tell yourself about it. As mentioned in the previous chapter, this action opens the door to dark forces.

If the stone's power depends on your belief, what happens when your belief falters?

The Ancient Warning

The Bible often warns against trusting in objects for power. Not because objects are evil, but because they can't carry the weight we put on them.

“Their land is full of idols; they bow down to the work of their hands, to what their fingers have made.” — Isaiah 2:8 (NIV)

The danger isn’t the stone itself—it’s the misplaced hope.

The Gospel and the True Source of Power

Christianity doesn’t deny beauty in creation. Crystals, like stars, declare glory—but they don’t define destiny. They can reflect wonder, but they can’t restore hearts.

Power isn’t in the stone. It’s in the One who spoke the stone into being.

“For from him and through him and for him are all things. To him be the glory forever! Amen.” — Romans 11:36 (NIV)

The Shift

You don’t need rose quartz to be loved. You don’t need amethyst to find peace. You don’t need citrine to unlock abundance.

What if the beauty of the stone is a signpost, not a source? What if the shimmer points beyond itself to the One who made it? What if the power you seek isn’t in your hand, but in His?

The glow of crystals fades. The glory of God endures.

CHAPTER 13: YOGA AND THE SEARCH FOR UNION — WHY STRETCHING CAN'T SAVE YOUR SOUL

Introduction: More Than Exercise

For many in the West, yoga begins as exercise. It promises flexibility, calm, and stress relief. But for others, it becomes more than stretching—it becomes a spiritual path.

The word *yoga* means "union." The goal isn't just health, but transcendence: dissolving the self into the divine, awakening hidden energies, and achieving enlightenment.

At first, this sounds harmless—even beautiful. But the deeper you go, the more you realize yoga isn't just about poses. It's about a worldview.

The Appeal of Embodied Spirituality

Yoga resonates because it connects body and spirit. In a fragmented world, it feels holistic. Breath, posture, and meditation combine into a ritual of presence.

"I started yoga for back pain. But soon, the teacher was talking about chakras, mantras, and awakening kundalini energy. I wasn't just stretching anymore—I was being invited into a spiritual system."

The appeal is real: it feels like healing. But the question is—healing into what?

The Spiritual Roots

Yoga is rooted in Hindu philosophy. Its ultimate aim is liberation (*moksha*)—escaping the cycle of rebirth by realizing your oneness with Brahman, the divine essence of all things.

This is why many yoga practices include chanting, mantras, and meditation on deities. The poses are not neutral—they were historically acts of worship.

Philosopher Huston Smith observed: *"Yoga is not merely physical exercise. It is a spiritual discipline designed to lead the practitioner to union with the divine."*

If the goal is union with the divine essence, what happens to the distinction between Creator and creation?

The Western Rebrand

In the West, yoga is often stripped of its overt spirituality and marketed as wellness. Studios advertise it as stress relief, mindfulness, or even "Christian yoga."

But even when rebranded, the underlying philosophy often seeps through. Breathwork becomes energy work. Poses become portals. Meditation becomes mantra.

This doesn't mean every yoga class is a covert religious ritual. But it does mean the practice carries a worldview—one that may not align with the Gospel.

The Problem of Self-Deification

At its core, yoga teaches that divinity is within you, waiting to be awakened. Salvation is not received, but realized. You don't need grace—you need awareness.

This sounds empowering, but it places the burden on you. If you fail to awaken, you fail spiritually. If you can't ascend, you're stuck.

What kind of salvation depends on your flexibility?

The Biblical Contrast: Rest, Not Ascent

The Bible offers a different vision of body and spirit. It doesn't deny embodiment—it affirms it. But instead of dissolving the self into the divine, it calls you into relationship with the divine.

"Do you not know that your bodies are temples of the Holy Spirit, who is in you, whom you have received from God?" — 1 Corinthians 6:19 (NIV)

Union in Christianity is not absorption into God, but communion with Him. Not self-deification, but indwelling. Not striving upward, but receiving downward grace.

The Shift

You don't need to awaken hidden energy. You don't need to dissolve into the divine. You don't need to stretch your way into salvation.

What if peace isn't found in union with everything, but in communion with Someone? What if freedom isn't about dissolving the self, but being fully known and fully loved? What if the rest you long for isn't in a pose, but in a Person?

The shimmer of yoga fades. The presence of God endures.

CHAPTER 14: MEDITATION AND MINDFULNESS — WHY EMPTYING YOURSELF ISN'T ENOUGH

Introduction: The Promise of Peace

"Be present." "Empty your mind." "Detach from your thoughts."

Meditation and mindfulness promise calm in a chaotic world. They offer techniques to slow down, breathe, and notice. For many, they bring real relief from stress and anxiety.

But beneath the stillness lies a question: if peace depends on emptying yourself, what fills the space when you're done?

The Appeal of Mindfulness

Mindfulness resonates because it works—at least in part. Breathing slows the body. Focus interrupts distraction. Silence feels like a reset.

"I started mindfulness meditation during a stressful season at work. Sitting quietly, focusing on my breath, helped me calm down. But when I got up from the cushion, the same problems were waiting. The peace didn't last."

The practice soothes, but it doesn't solve.

The Roots of Meditation

Modern mindfulness is often presented as secular, but its roots lie in Buddhist philosophy. The goal is detachment—freedom from desire, ego, and self. By emptying the mind, you dissolve attachment and find release.

This can sound noble, but it raises a question: if the self is the problem, what's left when the self is gone?

The Western Rebrand

In the West, mindfulness has been rebranded as productivity. Corporations teach it to employees to reduce stress and increase focus. Apps sell it as a subscription. Schools use it to calm restless students.

But when mindfulness becomes a tool for efficiency, it loses its soul. Instead of liberation, it becomes optimization. Instead of freedom, it becomes performance.

What kind of peace is it if it only makes you a better worker bee?

The Limits of Emptying

Emptying the mind can bring temporary relief, but it cannot provide lasting meaning. Silence can calm, but it cannot guide. Detachment can soothe, but it cannot love.

The Bible offers a different vision: not emptying, but filling. Not detachment, but communion.

"Do not get drunk on wine, which leads to debauchery. Instead, be filled with the Spirit." — Ephesians 5:18 (NIV)

The goal is not to erase the self, but to renew it. Not to detach from desire, but to redirect it toward the One who satisfies.

The Shift

You don't need to empty yourself into silence. You don't need to detach until nothing remains. You don't need to chase peace that fades when the timer ends.

What if peace isn't the absence of thought, but the presence of Someone? What if freedom isn't detachment, but communion? What if the stillness you long for isn't found in emptiness, but in fullness?

The calm of mindfulness fades. The presence of God endures.

CHAPTER 15: PSYCHEDELICS AND PLANT MEDICINE — WHY VISIONS CAN'T HEAL YOU

Introduction: The Promise of the Brew

Ayahuasca. San Pedro. Psilocybin.

Plant medicine ceremonies promise breakthrough. They offer visions, catharsis, and connection to the divine. Participants describe journeys of light, shadow, and revelation.

But beneath the visions lies a sobering reality: the trip ends, and the ache remains.

The Appeal of Psychedelic Healing

Psychedelics resonate because they feel transcendent. They dissolve boundaries, unlock emotions, and create a sense of unity.

"I drank ayahuasca in the jungle. The visions were overwhelming—colors, voices, memories. For a moment, I felt like I touched eternity. But when I came home, the depression was still there. The visions didn't fix it."

The experience is powerful. But power isn't the same as healing.

The Marketplace of Mysticism

Plant medicine has become a global industry, including essential oils. Retreats charge thousands for ceremonies led by shamans or facilitators. The promise is always the same: "This will change your life."

But the cycle often repeats. One ceremony leads to another. One breakthrough demands the next. Healing becomes a subscription, not a solution.

Anthropologist Michael Winkelman notes: *"Psychedelics can induce profound experiences, but without integration, they often fail to produce lasting transformation."*

What kind of healing requires endless repetition?

The Problem of Visions

Visions can feel divine, but they are not always reliable. They can contradict, confuse, or overwhelm. They can expose wounds without healing them.

Some participants report terrifying experiences—encounters with darkness, despair, or chaos. Others chase the high, hoping the next vision will finally deliver peace.

But visions, however vivid, cannot carry the weight of salvation.

The Biblical Contrast: Revelation, Not Hallucination

The Bible doesn't deny visions. Prophets saw them. Apostles experienced them. But biblical visions were not induced—they were given. They weren't sought through substances, but received through relationship.

"In the last days, God says, I will pour out my Spirit on all people. Your sons and daughters will prophesy, your young men will see visions, your old men will dream dreams." — Acts 2:17 (NIV)

The difference is crucial: psychedelic visions come from plants; biblical visions come from God. One fades with the chemical. The other endures with the Spirit.

The Weight of Escapism

For many, psychedelics become a way to escape pain rather than face it. The visions distract, but they don't deliver. The ceremony feels like progress, but the wounds remain.

"I kept going back to ceremonies, thinking the next one would finally heal me. But each time, I came home to the same emptiness. The visions were intense, but they didn't change my life."

What if the breakthrough you're chasing isn't in a vision, but in a voice?

The Shift

You don't need another ceremony. You don't need another vision. You don't need another trip into the unknown.

What if healing isn't found in hallucination, but in revelation? What if peace isn't in a plant, but in a Person? What if the freedom you long for isn't in altered states, but in a steady Savior?

The shimmer of visions fades. The Word endures.

CHAPTER 16: ANGELS, ALIENS, AND ASCENDED MASTERS — WHY COUNTERFEIT LIGHT CAN'T SAVE YOU

Introduction: Messengers of Light

"Your guardian angel is guiding you." "An ascended master is speaking through me." "Aliens seeded humanity and are returning to awaken us."

These claims sound transcendent. They promise wisdom from beyond, guidance from higher beings, and comfort in a chaotic world. They shimmer with mystery.

But the question remains: how do you know which voices are true—and which are counterfeit?

The Appeal of Higher Beings

The idea of angels, aliens, or ascended masters resonates because it lifts us out of isolation. You're not alone—there are beings watching, guiding, and empowering you.

"I went to a channeling circle where someone claimed to speak with Archangel Michael. The words were comforting, but they sounded suspiciously like things I'd already told the group earlier. I left wondering—was it really Michael, or just an echo of my own hopes? Or some evil being imitating Michael?"

The longing is real. But longing can be manipulated.

The Problem of Counterfeit Light

Not every being that claims to be light is trustworthy. Some flatter, some confuse, some deceive.

The Bible warns:

"Satan himself masquerades as an angel of light." — 2 Corinthians 11:14 (NIV)

This doesn't mean every spiritual encounter is demonic. But it does mean discernment is essential. If every voice is affirmed, then deception is inevitable.

Aliens and the Myth of Cosmic Origins

In some circles, aliens are framed as humanity's creators or saviors. Ancient astronaut theories suggest we were seeded by extraterrestrials and are now being guided back to cosmic unity.

At first, this feels thrilling—like we're part of a bigger story. But it also reduces humanity to an experiment and salvation to technology.

Philosopher Peter Kreeft once remarked: *"If we are only the product of cosmic accidents or alien interventions, then our dignity is diminished. But if we are created in the image of God, our worth is immeasurable."*

Ascended Masters and the Burden of Hierarchy

The teaching of ascended masters—enlightened beings who guide humanity—creates a spiritual hierarchy. Some are "further along," others are "less evolved."

This can inspire, but it can also oppress. If you're struggling, you're told you're not evolved enough. If you doubt, you're told you're not awakened. Instead of freedom, you're given pressure.

What kind of love ranks you on a cosmic ladder?

The Biblical Contrast: One Mediator

The Bible acknowledges angels, but it never asks us to worship or channel them. Their role is to serve, not to save.

"For there is one God and one mediator between God and mankind, the man Christ Jesus." — 1 Timothy 2:5 (NIV)

The Gospel doesn't multiply mediators—it simplifies them. You don't need angels, aliens, or ascended masters to reach God. You need Jesus.

The Shift

You don't need another messenger. You don't need another master. You don't need another voice that flatters but cannot free.

What if the light you need isn't counterfeit, but true? What if the guide you long for isn't distant, but near? What if the mediator you seek isn't many, but one?

The shimmer of counterfeit light fades. The true Light endures.

"I am the light of the world. Whoever follows me will never walk in darkness, but will have the light of life." — John 8:12 (NIV)

CHAPTER 17: DEATH, MEDIUMS, AND THE AFTERLIFE — WHY THE DEAD DON'T SPEAK BUT HOPE STILL LIVES

Introduction: The Ache of Loss

When someone you love dies, the silence is unbearable. You long for one more word, one more sign, one more glimpse. Mediums and afterlife guides step into that ache, offering connection with the departed.

It feels compassionate. It feels healing. It feels like hope.

But the question remains: if the dead are speaking, why do the messages sound so much like us?

The Appeal of Mediumship

Mediums promise what grief craves: contact. They offer words of comfort, closure, and reassurance.

"I went to a medium after my father died. She told me he was proud of me, that he was watching over me. It was exactly what I wanted to hear. But later, I wondered—was it really him, or just what anyone grieving would long to hear?"

The comfort is real. But is the source?

The Problem of Vagueness

Mediumship often relies on generalities:

- "He's proud of you."

- “She’s at peace.”
- “They’re sending love.”

These statements resonate because they’re universally comforting. Psychologists call this the **Barnum effect**—the tendency to accept vague, flattering statements as uniquely personal.

The result? You feel seen, but not necessarily spoken to.

The Danger of Deception

Not all voices are benign. Some flatter, some confuse, some manipulate. The Bible warns:

“Do not turn to mediums or seek out spiritists, for you will be defiled by them. I am the Lord your God.” — Leviticus 19:31 (NIV)

The danger isn’t just fraud—it’s spiritual vulnerability. When you open yourself to any voice, you risk hearing the wrong one.

The Ache That Remains

Even when a medium’s words bring comfort, the ache doesn’t vanish. The longing remains. The empty chair is still empty. The silence still echoes.

“I left the séance feeling lighter. But the next morning, the grief was back. The words hadn’t filled the void—they had only delayed it.”

What kind of hope fades overnight?

The Biblical Contrast: A Living Hope

Christianity doesn't deny grief. It names it. It doesn't silence tears. It sanctifies them. But it also offers something mediums cannot: a living hope.

"Brothers and sisters, we do not want you to be uninformed about those who sleep in death, so that you do not grieve like the rest of mankind, who have no hope." — 1 Thessalonians 4:13 (NIV)

The promise isn't that the dead speak now, but that the dead will rise then. Not vague reassurances, but a concrete resurrection.

The Shift

You don't need another séance. You don't need another vague reassurance. You don't need another voice that cannot anchor.

What if the hope you need isn't in whispers from the dead, but in a word from the Living? What if the comfort you long for isn't in messages, but in resurrection? What if the silence of death isn't the end, but the pause before a greater song?

The shimmer of mediums fades. The hope of resurrection endures.

PART III: FINDING REALITY AND REST

Okay, we've diagnosed the ache and traced the shadows. Now what if we told you there's an off-ramp? This is the **shift**. After exposing the broken promises, we pivot to the substance you've been starving for.

This part isn't about more striving; it's about **finished grace**. It's about the true, coherent **Reality** that eliminates the need for all the seeking, performance, and self-deification. Get ready for the peace that finally allows you to put the work down and **actually rest**.

CHAPTER 18: THE NEW AGE JESUS — WHY THE REAL CHRIST IS BETTER THAN THE COUNTERFEIT

Introduction: A Familiar Name, a Different Face

Walk into a New Age bookstore and you'll see Him everywhere. Jesus on oracle cards. Jesus in channeled messages. Jesus as a "cosmic ascended master."

The name is the same. The face looks familiar. But the message has been rewritten.

What happens when the most recognized figure in history is remade in our own image?

The New Age Jesus

In New Age spirituality, Jesus is often presented as:

- A wise teacher who discovered divine consciousness.
- A healer who tapped into universal energy.
- A model of enlightenment, not a Savior.

This version of Jesus is safe. He doesn't confront sin. He doesn't demand repentance. He doesn't die on a cross. He simply affirms your inner light.

"I loved the New Age Jesus because he never disagreed with me. He was always affirming, always gentle, always vague. But over time, I realized he sounded suspiciously like... me."

The Problem of a Tamed Christ

A Jesus who never confronts is a Jesus who never saves. If He only reflects your desires, He cannot redeem your failures. If He only affirms your truth, He cannot rescue you from lies.

Theologian N.T. Wright warns: *"If you dethrone the Jesus of history and replace him with a figure of your own imagination, you are left with a projection, not a person."*

What kind of Savior never disagrees with you?

The Historical Christ

The real Jesus of history is not vague. He is specific. He claimed authority, demanded allegiance, and offered forgiveness.

- He called Himself the Son of God (John 10:36).
- He forgave sins (Mark 2:5–7).
- He predicted His death and resurrection (Mark 8:31).

These are not the claims of a mere teacher. They are the claims of a Lord.

The Cross at the Center

The New Age Jesus skips the cross. But without the cross, there is no Gospel.

"For the message of the cross is foolishness to those who are perishing, but to us who are being saved it is the power of God." — 1 Corinthians 1:18 (NIV)

The real Jesus doesn't just affirm your light. He enters your darkness. He doesn't just model enlightenment. He bears your sin. He doesn't just inspire. He saves.

The Living Christ

The counterfeit Jesus is endlessly adaptable—He changes with the culture. But the real Christ is alive, unchanging, and reigning.

"Jesus Christ is the same yesterday and today and forever." — Hebrews 13:8 (NIV)

The counterfeit comforts. The real Christ transforms.

The Shift

You don't need another guru. You don't need another ascended master. You don't need another projection of yourself.

What if the Jesus you've been offered is too small? What if the real Christ is not just a teacher, but a Savior? What if the hope you long for isn't in a counterfeit, but in the living Lord?

The shimmer of the New Age Jesus fades. The power of the risen Christ endures.

CHAPTER 19: UNITY OR DIVISION? — WHY TRUE ONENESS REQUIRES TRUTH

Introduction: The Dream of Oneness

"Everything is one." "We're all connected." "Unity is the highest vibration."

The New Age vision of unity is compelling. It promises harmony, dissolves difference, and offers belonging. In a fractured world, who wouldn't want that?

But beneath the dream lies a dilemma: if unity ignores truth, is it really unity—or just a fragile truce?

The Appeal of Cosmic Oneness

The language of oneness resonates because it speaks to our longing for connection. We're tired of division, weary of conflict, and hungry for belonging.

"I joined a spiritual community that preached oneness. At first, it felt healing—no judgment, no labels, just love. But when I started asking hard questions about truth, I was told I was being 'divisive.' Unity was welcome—until it required honesty."

The promise of oneness is real. But it often comes at the cost of truth.

The Problem of Shallow Unity

When unity is built on ignoring differences, it becomes fragile.

- Disagreement is silenced in the name of harmony.
- Truth claims are dismissed as "low-vibe."
- Conviction is reframed as intolerance.

The result? A community that looks united but is actually brittle. The moment real conflict arises, the unity shatters.

Sociologist Christian Smith observes: *"A culture of tolerance without truth produces fragility, not strength. It cannot withstand the weight of real difference."*

What kind of unity collapses the moment it's tested?

The Hidden Elitism of "Oneness"

Ironically, movements that preach oneness often create new divisions. Those who "get it" are enlightened. Those who question are asleep. Those who doubt are toxic.

Instead of dissolving hierarchy, oneness creates a new one—those who are "high-vibe" versus those who are not.

"I was told we were all one, but when I struggled with depression, I was told my energy was dragging the group down. Suddenly, I wasn't included in the oneness anymore."

The Biblical Contrast: Unity in Truth

The Bible doesn't dismiss unity—it commands it. But it roots unity in truth, not in denial.

"Make every effort to keep the unity of the Spirit through the bond of peace. There is one body and one Spirit… one Lord, one faith, one baptism; one God and Father of all." — Ephesians 4:3–6 (NIV)

Christian unity doesn't erase difference—it reconciles it. It doesn't silence conviction—it anchors it. It doesn't demand sameness—it celebrates diversity under one Lord.

The Shift

You don't need unity that silences you. You don't need oneness that excludes you. You don't need harmony that hides the truth.

What if true unity isn't found in dissolving difference, but in reconciling it? What if belonging isn't about sameness, but about being known and loved in truth? What if the oneness you long for isn't cosmic, but Christ-centered?

The shimmer of shallow unity fades. The strength of truth-filled unity endures.

CHAPTER 20: THE END OF THE AGE — WHY HOPE IS MORE THAN A VIBRATION

Introduction: The Forecast of Fear

Scroll through New Age forums and you'll see it everywhere: "The Age of Aquarius is dawning." "Humanity is ascending." "Cosmic shifts are coming."

The end of the age is framed as a vibration upgrade—a planetary awakening. It promises light, unity, and transcendence. But it also stirs fear: if you're not aligned, you'll be left behind.

What happens when your hope depends on keeping up with the cosmos?

The Appeal of Cosmic Timelines

New Age eschatology resonates because it gives meaning to chaos. Wars, disasters, and crises are reframed as "birth pangs" of a new age. Instead of despair, you're told to expect transformation.

"I was told 2012 would be the great shift. I meditated, fasted, and prepared. But when nothing happened, I felt foolish. Then the date was moved to 2020. Then 2030. The hope kept shifting, but the ache remained."

The timeline comforts, but it also disappoints.

The Problem of Moving Goalposts

Predictions of cosmic shifts rarely deliver. When the date passes, the narrative adapts:

- "The shift was invisible."
- "The vibration is still rising."
- "The real change is coming soon."

The goalposts move, but the anxiety stays. Instead of peace, you're left with perpetual waiting.

Sociologist Leon Festinger, who studied failed prophecies, observed: *"When prophecy fails, believers often double down, not abandon the belief. Hope becomes harder to let go of than truth."*

What kind of hope always delays itself?

The Weight of Fear

New Age end-times teaching often carries an undercurrent of fear. If you're not "high-vibe," you'll miss the shift. If you're not awakened, you'll be left behind.

Instead of assurance, you're given pressure. Instead of peace, you're given panic.

"I lived in constant fear that I wasn't aligned enough. Every bad mood felt like a cosmic failure. Instead of hope, I felt haunted."

The Biblical Contrast: A Certain Hope

The Bible also speaks of the end of the age. But instead of vibrations, it speaks of a Person. Instead of shifting timelines, it speaks of a certain return.

“So Christ was sacrificed once to take away the sins of many; and he will appear a second time, not to bear sin, but to bring salvation to those who are waiting for him.” — Hebrews 9:28 (NIV)

The difference is striking:

- New Age hope is fragile, tied to shifting dates.
- Christian hope is anchored, tied to a faithful Savior.

The Living Hope

Christian hope is not vague optimism. It is resurrection hope. It doesn’t depend on your vibration, but on His victory.

“Praise be to the God and Father of our Lord Jesus Christ! In his great mercy he has given us new birth into a living hope through the resurrection of Jesus Christ from the dead.” — 1 Peter 1:3 (NIV)

This hope doesn’t shift with the stars. It stands with the cross.

The Shift

You don’t need another prophecy date. You don’t need another vibration upgrade. You don’t need another cosmic forecast.

What if hope isn’t about aligning with the stars, but trusting the One who made them? What if the end of the age isn’t a vibration, but a visitation? What if the future you long for isn’t fragile, but finished?

The shimmer of cosmic timelines fades. The living hope endures.

CHAPTER 21: FROM SHADOWS TO SUBSTANCE — THE GOSPEL EXPLAINED

You've heard the slogans: "Raise your vibration." "Manifest your reality." "Find the divine within."

But what if the real story isn't about you climbing up, but about God coming down?

That's the difference between the shimmer of New Age and the substance of the Gospel. The Gospel isn't another technique, another ritual, or another subscription. It's not a vibe you curate or a truth you invent. It's an announcement—good news—that God has acted in history to rescue people like us.

And if you've ever wondered what Christianity actually teaches—not the Instagram version, not the caricature, not the church-hurt distortions—this is it.

God: Holy and Loving

The Bible doesn't start with us. It starts with God. Not "the universe," not "energy," not "Source." A personal God—holy, pure, radiant in justice and love.

"Holy, holy, holy is the Lord of hosts; the whole earth is full of his glory!" (Isaiah 6:3, ESV)

Holiness means He's not like us. He's set apart, perfect, blazing in moral beauty. And that holiness isn't cold—it's the fire of His love.

"God is love." (1 John 4:8, ESV)

"The holiness of God is the most difficult of all God's attributes to explain... Holiness is that which sets God apart." — R.C. Sproul

---

Us: The Problem We Can't Fix

If God is holy, then our problem isn't just stress, trauma, or "low vibes." It's sin. We can't attain God's perfection. Nothing we can do can reach it.

"For all have sinned and fall short of the glory of God." (Romans 3:23, ESV)

Sin isn't just breaking rules—it's breaking relationship. It's saying to the God who made us, "I'll run my own life. I will be god." And in doing that, I have hurt people and myself. That's why guilt lingers even after the rituals.

"For the wages of sin is death, but the free gift of God is eternal life in Christ Jesus our Lord." (Romans 6:23, ESV)

"Sin is cosmic treason... an act of supreme ingratitude toward the One to whom we owe everything." — R.C. Sproul

You can't heal yourself if you're the wound. You can't save yourself if you're the problem.

Jesus: The Rescue We Couldn't Imagine

Here's the turning point. God doesn't leave us in the dark. He loves us so much that He comes down.

"The Word became flesh and dwelt among us." (John 1:14, ESV)

Jesus Christ isn't another guru. He is God in the flesh.

And He didn't come just to inspire. He came to substitute.

"But he was pierced for our transgressions; he was crushed for our iniquities." (Isaiah 53:5, ESV)

That's penal substitution: In God's court of justice, we deserve a punishment of death, but He took our place.

"For our sake he made him to be sin who knew no sin, so that in him we might become the righteousness of God." (2 Corinthians 5:21, ESV)

This isn't karma. Karma says you pay what you owe. The cross says Jesus paid it all. This isn't manifestation. Manifestation says you create your reality. The resurrection says God raised Jesus from the dead.

"He is not here, for he has risen, as he said." (Matthew 28:6, ESV)

"The heart of the gospel is this: Jesus Christ died for our sins and was raised for our justification." — John Stott

---

The Call to Respond

The Gospel isn't just information—it's an invitation.

"Repent therefore, and turn back, that your sins may be blotted out." (Acts 3:19, ESV)

Repentance isn't self-improvement. It's turning from self to God. Faith isn't a vague belief. It's trust in Jesus' finished work.

"For by grace you have been saved through faith. And this is not your own doing; it is the gift of God." (Ephesians 2:8, ESV)

"Faith is the empty hand that receives the gift of God's grace." — Charles Spurgeon

---

The Spirit's Work

The Holy Spirit doesn't just "activate energy." He gives new life.

"That which is born of the flesh is flesh, and that which is born of the Spirit is spirit." (John 3:6, ESV)

He reshapes us into Christ's likeness. When we repent, accept that God has provided the way to Him, that we can't do it on our own, then He gives calls us His children. He sees you as holy, perfect, and pure, and that can't be taken away.

"We… are being transformed into the same image from one degree of glory to another." (2 Corinthians 3:18, ESV)

He dwells in believers, guiding, convicting, comforting.

"The Spirit himself bears witness with our spirit that we are children of God." (Romans 8:16, ESV)

Walking in the Light

The Christian life isn't endless striving. It's daily faith, repentance, and joy in Christ.

"If we walk in the light, as he is in the light, we have fellowship with one another." (1 John 1:7, ESV)

Belonging isn't based on alignment or vibe. It's adoption into God's family.

"See what kind of love the Father has given to us, that we should be called children of God." (1 John 3:1, ESV)

And hope isn't reincarnation or karmic cycles. It's resurrection and eternal life.

"According to his great mercy, he has caused us to be born again to a living hope through the resurrection of Jesus Christ." (1 Peter 1:3, ESV)

"The gospel is not just the ABCs of the Christian life, it is the A to Z." — Tim Keller

---

The Contrast Made Clear

- New Age: self as source, endless striving, temporary highs.
- Gospel: God as source, finished work, lasting peace.

"Come to me, all who labor and are heavy laden, and I will give you rest." (Matthew 11:28, ESV)

Not self-ascent, but Christ's descent. Not awakening, but rescue. Not fragments, but the whole story.

Invitation

If you've felt the ache, if you've chased the shimmer, if you've tried to curate your own divinity and still ended up empty—this is the moment to see the difference.

The Gospel isn't about you finding your way to God. It's about God finding His way to you.

"But God shows his love for us in that while we were still sinners, Christ died for us." (Romans 5:8, ESV)

A Prayer of Repentance and Faith

If you've reached this point and you want to turn from shadows to substance, here is a prayer you can make your own. The words themselves don't save you—Jesus does. But this prayer can help you put into words the posture of your heart:

"Holy God, I confess that I have sinned against You. I have tried to live as my own source, and I cannot save myself. I repent for my life of rebellion against You, and for the hurt I have caused. I turn from my sin and place my trust in Jesus Christ, who died in my place and rose again to give me life. Thank you for forgiving me, cleansing me, and making me new. Thank you for filling me with Your Spirit so that I may walk in faith, follow You as Lord, and live as Your child. Thank You for Your grace and for the gift of eternal life. Thank you for loving me. In Jesus' name, Amen."

The Shift

- From chasing vibes → to receiving truth.
- From endless striving → to resting in grace.
- From shadows → to substance.

EPILOGUE: STEPPING OUT OF THE SHADOWS

You've walked through the shimmer. You imagined hope. You've seen the promises of New Age spirituality—its rituals, its language, its beauty—and you've seen how quickly the glow fades. You've also seen the substance of the Gospel: not another cycle, not another subscription, but a finished rescue.

But the story doesn't end there. It ends with a choice.

Every generation has to decide what to do with *the light*. Some admire it from a distance. Some dabble in it while still chasing shadows. And some step into it fully, letting it change everything.

The ache you've felt—the one that drove you to search, to experiment, to keep reaching for more—isn't a flaw. It's a signal. It's the echo of eternity in your soul, pointing you beyond yourself.

"The light shines in the darkness, and the darkness has not overcome it." (John 1:5, ESV)

The invitation is not just to leave behind counterfeits. It's to step into a life that lasts. A life where you are known, forgiven, and loved. A life where your scars don't define you, but testify to grace. A life where hope isn't fragile, but anchored.

This is not about winning arguments. It's about finding rest. It's about trading the endless loop of striving for the steady voice of a Shepherd who calls you by name.

And it's about more than you. The light you step into is not just for your healing—it's for your generation. For your friends who are still caught in the loop. For your community that is still chasing shimmer. For a world that is still restless in the dark.

So here, at the end of this book, the invitation is simple: Don't just admire the light. Walk in it. Share it. Let it shine through you.

Because the shadows are many. The shimmer is strong. But the light is stronger still.

"For once you were darkness, but now you are light in the Lord. Walk as children of light." (Ephesians 5:8, ESV)

.

REFERENCES

General Surveys of the New Age Movement

- **Douglas Groothuis.** *Unmasking the New Age.* Downers Grove, IL: InterVarsity Press, 1986.
- **Douglas Groothuis.** *Confronting the New Age.* Downers Grove, IL: InterVarsity Press, 1988.
- **Elliot Miller.** *A Crash Course on the New Age Movement.* Grand Rapids, MI: Baker Book House, 1989.
- **John Ankerberg and John Weldon.** *The Facts on the New Age Movement.* Eugene, OR: Harvest House, 1988.

Philosophical and Theological Critiques

- **Peter Jones.** *The Gnostic Empire Strikes Back: An Old Heresy for the New Age.* Phillipsburg, NJ: Presbyterian & Reformed, 1992.
- **Peter Jones.** *Spirit Wars: Pagan Revival in Christian America.* Mukilteo, WA: WinePress, 1997.
- **Peter Jones.** *The Other Worldview: Exposing Christianity's Greatest Threat.* Bellingham, WA: Kirkdale Press, 2015.
- **Carl F. H. Henry.** *God, Revelation, and Authority.* Vol. 1–6. Waco, TX: Word, 1976–1983. (For grounding in revelation vs. relativism).

Historical and Gnostic Roots

- **Ronald H. Nash.** *Christianity and the Hellenistic World.* Grand Rapids, MI: Zondervan, 1984.
- **Ronald H. Nash.** *The Gospel and the Greeks: Did the New Testament Borrow from Pagan Thought?* Phillipsburg, NJ: Presbyterian & Reformed, 1992.
- **Philip J. Lee.** *Against the Protestant Gnostics.* New York: Oxford University Press, 1987.

Occult Practices and Spiritual Counterfeits

- **Walter Martin.** *The Kingdom of the Cults.* Minneapolis, MN: Bethany House, rev. ed. 2003.
- **John Ankerberg and John Weldon.** *The Facts on Astrology.* Eugene, OR: Harvest House, 1988.
- **John Ankerberg and John Weldon.** *The Facts on Spirit Guides.* Eugene, OR: Harvest House, 1991.

Apologetics and Cultural Engagement

- **Francis A. Schaeffer.** *The God Who Is There.* Downers Grove, IL: InterVarsity Press, 1968.
- **Francis A. Schaeffer.** *Escape from Reason.* Downers Grove, IL: InterVarsity Press, 1968.
- **Alisa Childers.** *Another Gospel? A Lifelong Christian Seeks Truth in Response to Progressive Christianity.* Carol Stream, IL: Tyndale, 2020. (Helpful for modern parallels).
- **James W. Sire.** *The Universe Next Door: A Basic Worldview Catalog.* Downers Grove, IL: InterVarsity Press, 1976; multiple updated editions.

Made in the USA
Coppell, TX
18 February 2026